Why Do We Know But Live Like We Don't

By

Ricky Barton

Copyright © 2025 by Ricky Barton

All rights reserved. No part of this book may be reproduced, distributed, or transmitted in any form or by any means, including photocopying, recording, or other electronic or mechanical methods, without the prior written permission of the publisher, except in the case of brief quotations embodied in critical reviews and certain other non-commercial uses permitted by copyright law.

Dedication

To my mother and Father for always telling me You Know Better

My two children, my grand and great-grandchildren,

All my sisters and brothers for always pushing me to be better

To STX where the will of God happened

To God, for he is all the glory

TGBTG

Acknowledgment

I am deeply grateful to my now good friend Ivan Garcia for his timely knudge And his attention to detail.

Ivan made my experience as a first-time arthur much more exciting than I really thought. Massive thank you, my friend Ivan Garcia.

This book was written first for me to change me. But as I wrote, I felt like I was standing in front of a BIG mirror, and as I saw changes, some family members suggested sharing my experience.

I would like to say thank you to my sisters, the eldest, for her example with education.

My middle sis for always thinking big and living just as big.

My baby sis for being who she is, God fearing and loving, to know her is to love her.

And for all my Grands for always showing me unconditional love.

TGBTG

About the Author

I am Ricky Barton, a child of the Most High God.

My God has allowed me to live an exceptional life, which was marred for 36 years.

Raised a few kids, two of my own, and enjoyed four grand and one great grand

I served in the US Army and owned a few businesses

I now live in the most amazing place and am learning to love my neighbors as I love myself.

This is my first of many books

And for me, it is only God's will that will be done.

TGBTG

Table of Contents

Chapter One: Because You Know This 1

Chapter Two: Mentality Leads 8

Chapter Three: Believing 16

Chapter Four: Learn to Listen So You Listen to Learn 22

Chapter Five: Time and Timing 31

Chapter Six: Family and Relationship 40

Chapter Seven: Wisdom, Knowledge, and Understanding 47

Chapter Eight: Minor Adjustment 54

Chapter Nine: Permission to Start 62

Chapter Ten: You Really Do Know 69

Chapter One: Because You Know This

Both you and I know that if you put one dollar away every day, at the end of that year, you would have $365. Because we know, then we should break it down to be edible and doable. One week, you can find $7—That's one coffee a week. In one month, you can find $28—That's one eat-out a month. In six months, you can have $168.

By this time, you are well into your new habit of three weeks (21 days). And you can improve—even if it's just thinking about how to compound your efforts, which only adds more to your new game.

I was a pretty decent basketball player, but as I got older, I decreased in some areas, like driving to the hoop and taking hard fouls, because getting up was harder than the actual foul. I had to adjust.

To me, my adjustment made my three-pointer better. That was a well-deserved compounding on my shot and my body.

Our lives are full of many minor adjustments that make us different from years ago. I believe what you can control, you control to your best ability, and what you can't, you leave to God.

You know the results you want in life. You must make a decision, because we know and have heard that you must save for a rainy day. We complicate that idea by never starting.

You know that if you never start, you never finish. You know that if you pay yourself first every paycheck, you will feel different about your hustle. You know that action speaks louder than words. You know that you must put one foot in front of the other in order to go. You must go to the computer to apply for that hustle. You must go to the car to drive to your hustle. You know you must. Go to sleep.

The things we know that we know could change our lives are called decisions. When or why do you make that decision? At this stage, no one but you knows.

Decisions

When you make a decision, you will live with it. You will never forget a decision you made that changed your life. Yes, I'm talking about when you consciously make a decision—like doing adult things and becoming a Mom or a Dad. Like taking on a hustle you know you do not like. Like speaking about life but not living the way you speak.

We make a decision to go to school—to educate ourselves, to get ahead, to seek more, to get a better hustle, to build confidence, or just to know more.

We made a decision to get married, because the Bible told us that a man or woman should not live alone. A man should leave his parents' house and find a wife, which is a good thing. That's why God made Eve from Adam's rib—to give him a helpmate.

We make a decision to want more. You start dreaming and believing. If they can do it, I can too.

We make a decision to trust God—because you know God is the only way. Because He said, I will not leave you or forsake you. We know that with God, anything is possible. Lean not on your own understanding. His ways are not our ways. Ask, and it will be given.

We made a decision to renew our minds, because the same mind that got you here needs some renewing to fit your dreams. Renewing your mind is education for your new beginning.

We made a decision to motivate ourselves—because everything starts with you. Only you know your dreams. Only you want what you want. And only you know how much effort you are willing to give to yourself for your dreams and/or lifestyle.

This is how important making a decision is.

Start small. Start trusting in God—because He said, Seek ye first the kingdom of God. He also said, Seek and you will find—not might find, but will find. Then he said, Ask and it will be given. Again—it WILL be given. Then he said, You have not because you asked not.

I can go on and on about how the Bible helps you to take God at His word and trust. Him. Lean not on your own understanding, because God's ways are not our ways. He said, You know, I will always be with you.

Start by really wanting your dreams and believing you can have all that you can think or imagine. That is preparing your mind to be renewed, to be motivated to accomplish, to complete, and to become who you want to be.

That decision was, for me, the most important.

So I researched what renew means... to me, it meant being willing to change to improve one's mentality. Make a decision to put away $1 a day to start your journey of adjusting with practice.

In the chapter, we can discuss the importance of practice. You are ready to renew your mind because you believe you are ready. Honestly, if you change nothing, why would you expect anything to have changed?

My belief is that if you can focus on renewing your mind, your life will change. Stay positive. This is the day the Lord has made, and I will be glad in it.

Believe in yourself first..Trust—trust the gifts and talents that were placed in you.Seek—seek, and you will find... will find.

What you practice is what you become

You become more confident in yourself..You seek jobs that challenge you..You speak differently—because your circle changes.You speak to you differently..Quitting is not an option.

Your decision to become the person you want to be—you will feel it. Just pay attention to your dreams, your imagination, and the goals you think about daily. I believe our imagination created us as kids. Our goals guide us as we mature into adults. Our dreams pull us because we become leaders, parents, and we say to the kids:

"Dreams do come true. It can happen to you—IF YOU JUST BELIEVE."

You start believing your dreams because you see them so much in your mind. You must believe in yourself first.

Wrong and Right

Why do we know but live like we don't?

At one point in my life, I had to drive a car with no insurance or registration. Yes, I knew better—but I did it anyway because I was determined to change my situation. Because I knew it was wrong to do, every time I had to drive, the fear of the consequence loomed over my mind the whole time.

It was stressing me out so much that I was physically and mentally exhausted—and I made up my mind to change the type of fear.

Yes, I needed insurance and registration on the car, but I had the end in mind, and I did not have the resources to fix the car to get it registered, or the resources to insure the car. I was doing wrong to get to the right—bending the rules to make ends meet, robbing Peter to pay Paul.

While I drove the car, I was mentally scolding myself—and at the same time, I was excusing myself. And each of us knows that's not the way to live. That's confusing.

We can think of a few speeding consequences:

Speeding ticket- Accident- Someone dies- You die Another wrong—we can fix it with a decision.

1. Eating and its consequences

Overweight- Diabetes- Heart disease- Cancer

We know we can die from eating badly—we know that.

2. Our health and consequences

We do not exercise-We do not walk-Laziness- Addiction- Resting Of all the choices—why did you choose that one?

Because we know wrong from right, our choices will make or break us. You know that action speaks louder than words. You know that for every action there is a reaction. You know that your choices will determine the outcome.

We know—even doctors say rest is best for healing and growth. And we know—even Jesus rested.

Discipline yourself to abide by the rules again. What you practice is what you become.

Chapter Two: Mentality Leads

So I ask, why did I choose that one for me? The broken life was settling in, and I was not using my God-given gifts or what God has equipped me with. I always knew I was supposed to live the life God intended for me. He said it is his will that will be done. Trust in the Lord with all your heart; lean not on your own understanding.

I said to myself, You believe in God but not in what he put in you. Why? I truly believe it because to get rich, you have to do a little bit more consistently and dedicate yourself to something you believe in.

And really believe in it all the way. So that you do not say, Nah, I'll stay this way, you know that way has some regrets. That we hide, and they linger in our mind until we compartmentalize them and try to forget them, but nah, we still dream, we still imagine. And still want more for my life,

Your mind starts going to answer the question you ask yourself: Why trust and believe in God but not in what he put in you?? His ways are not our ways.

For years, we planned to retire and love our neighbors. I would pray and ask God to help me. Put in me the knowledge and wisdom to accomplish the desires of my heart. That you allow me to have. My beliefs, God said to me, I will help you because you ask. In the good book, it says, You have not because you do not ask. It also says, Ask and it will be given. I believe God said, I will give you a home, and all you ask for is the house. You must turn it into a home, then watch.

As the journey begins, I always wonder what God meant by the watch, but I trust and believe in God. So I packed up my entire life and followed what I believe God wants me to do in order for him to answer my prayers and his will that will be done. With God, I planned and planned for years.

To make this move, I even include a timeline to put my birthday in with all these accomplishments. Oh yes, I serve a big God, and his will be done.

We found a very nice fixer-upper in a very nice location, so we shipped everything we had for over 40 years to STX to retire and love our neighbors. God would be happy with that.

In STX, we lost that house. God said, I will see if you really trust or even believe me, but he armed me with his words. Do not worry, for worrying helps no one. So we found another home in the town I grew up in, where I became the young me I love looking back on.

Toby. But this was in the section as a young boy, I always dreamed of living in because they were the steps up to me…the house needed work. Remember, I was to turn it into a home, then watch. I keep seeing God's hands in everything.

From the selling of the three-family home we had, with one pic only, to the removal of old debt that to this day no one can find, everything, the smoothest move for me was going overseas.

God's hands even down to the house we bought—my neighbor was my big brother in such a way that I smoked my first joint from him. I honestly cry for days because of what God is doing.

I was curious what God meant by the watch, so every day I planned to turn that house into a home to see the watch God had for me. Each day, I would have something to do. While doing things around the house, I always listened to a few of my favorite songs. One of them was "I Have a Big God," because it speaks to the journey. A part of the song says:

"If you know my life, I so, so wonder, but if you know my God, He is a miracle worker."

Other songs had words like "I am next in line for my blessings." My playlist was full of praise music because I told myself, "I will praise my God with every breath I have."

When I was just about done turning the house into a home—upgrading the bathrooms, painting inside and out, setting the yard right—I felt like I was entering a mental slowdown to enjoy the rest of my life. But then,

God said the watch was to show me that His ways are not my ways—and He took it all away from me. He put me through the most pain I've ever felt in my life, just to tell me:

"You asked me for more. Live, and I will show you how."

GOD's ways are NOT our ways. I thank God every day for His will that will be done.

Mentality Leads

We know being broke is hard. We also know getting rich is hard. So why did you choose that one?

I used to think living paycheck to paycheck was horrible—but I told myself I was okay. My comfort zone kept me miserable—but I said I was okay. Skipping a bill or two each month felt normal. But then I thought: I've been doing this for years—and that is not OK.

That's when I started to analyze my conversations and the people around me who kept me mentally broken.. One of my friends would drive 8 miles just to save 15 cents. Make that make sense.

Another would say, No matter the game, I'm going to lose,"—coming in already defeated.

We should always remember.:If you think you can, you WILL. If you think you can't, you won't.Honestly, either way, you're 100% right.

I also believe I am exactly where I am in life because of all the choices I've made along the way. I stayed in places I knew I didn't belong for far too long. I trusted people I should have never let get close to me. I loved even when I knew the love was gone. I lived with people who did not value me or what God had blessed me with. I built with people who only wanted to break me down. I could go on, but we know—we are where our decisions have put us.

Practice

We all know that what we practice is what we become—or, better yet, what we get better at. When I heard that for the first time, it instantly clicked for me because I coached my son and the neighborhood kids. What sport do we know of that doesn't include practice before the season starts? And even when the season starts, they still practice.

We must practice anything we want to get good at—or even just enjoy. We can practice saving one dollar a day. We can practice following the law. We can practice treating people right. We can practice eating right. We can practice renewing our minds.

Most of us admire people who take their practice seriously and make a great living because of their dedication to becoming what they repeatedly do. If you half-practice, you get half the results. We all know how to practice—we've studied for tests, prepared for hustles.

It's like I watch you do your 50 sit-ups, and I only do 15—and still hope for your six-pack. How much you're willing to give to yourself is directly connected to what you can expect in return.

I was in the multilevel marketing business, and they told us what to do so we could be celebrated like the people on stage. Believe me, I saw people doing what they were supposed to do—dedicated to what they were willing to practice. For me, I knew I had to follow what worked, but I thought I could nonchalantly accomplish what they did for their level of achievement. That was my biggest mistake.

They said, "Practice doing these things, get better, and you should grow." I practiced only what I thought was easy and ignored what I thought was hard. I knew it had to work together, but I was half-stepping. I didn't grow—and I got bored with the business.

My nonchalant effort gave me a nonchalant return. I wanted what they had—but not the work they put in. A friend of mine had his picture on a billboard flexing. He said, "People want what I have, but not the work I put in to get it like this."

Hmm. What you practice becomes real. Your sweat, tears, and effort only mean something to YOU. We watch people who take practice seriously. What you practice is what you become. We even admire them—knowing we can do it too.

The business works—I saw it. I even enjoyed some spillover from those who practiced the right way.

Planning

Why do we know… but live like we don't?

We know planning works. We plan anything we believe is important. Like birthdays—we want them to be memorable. They only come once a year.

Trips—we pack, we triple-check everything, we plan every day down to the minute. We must know where to eat.

Weddings—whew, just the word "wedding" means spend and plan, then plan to plan the plan. Everything must be perfect: what you wear, where you sit, when you dance.

Even what we eat is planned.

Planning is very important to you—and you know it.

Chapter Three: Believing

We all know we must believe in something to give it the shot it needs. Let's start with—you must first believe in yourself. You would be very uncomfortable if you had to do anything you do not believe in. We go to higher education because we believe it will improve us. We go to work or hustle because we believe it will help us pay our bills and buy food to eat.

We believe in God and His words—the Basic Instructions Before Leaving Earth. We know and believe that we must trust it. The truth is, if you think you can, you will... if you think you can't, you won't. Some say they will try, but trying is not real in most senses. How do you try? To me, the word try is just a conversation piece that sounds good to the person saying it, because they believe it impresses the person hearing it. The non-existence of effort.

When you say try, I hear, I will put in just enough effort that I am comfortable with. But it is even more different than that... Well, try to sit or try to stand—and then point out the try—because you do or don't do it. You can't try to work; you work, or you don't work. You can't try to pay your bills; it's either you pay or you don't pay. You cannot half believe—so I believe you must believe in what you believe in.

One Rabbit

As a kid, my Dad always said, Focus on what you are doing. He was teaching me how important being focused is in life. He would say things like, If you are hungry, you should chase one rabbit. I do not know where he got that from, but it made sense to me. Because I always thought, if I were hungry, I would want to stock up so I wouldn't be hungry again.

But see, I know the right way is to focus on one meal—and then I can worry about stocking up. Just think, I am looking at the two fattest ones—I'm going to eat for days. I'm licking my lips, looking at them. Then the chase started. They both ran straight ahead. I got them in my sight and was just about to jump on them when one went east and the other went west. Whoo—what do I do? Go left or go right? Whoops, too late—I will remain hungry.

I know if I were focused on one, I would be eating. Knowing I cannot take step three before step one. But I was focused on the end. I would be eating for days, instead of eating today and recuperating for the next day. I always believed that if you want something, you must go for it. You must go for exactly what you want and believe you can get it.

When I tried to get rich, I knew I was half-stepping—but was expecting the big result. Yes, I said try—because I knew I was only going to give minimum effort. You must believe you are doing your best. You must believe you will give the effort needed to get the result you want. Make it easy on yourself and focus on one rabbit at a time.

The End in Mind

Everything you do starts with the end in mind. Before you made a decision to do anything, you thought about the reward, the result, and the accomplishment. You see yourself in victory lane many times before that decision is made. You go to school to further your education and open up more options for yourself—better hustle, better position, better pay.

You go to work only because it helps you live better. Pay your rent. Helps you buy a home. Helps you buy a car. Every one of those started with the end in mind. Let's see—to buy a home, you get tired of renting, tired of buying the house for someone else. When you start thinking of being a homeowner, you start looking at houses. Then you start to imagine yourself in your kitchen, in your yard, in the neighborhood you desire.

Why Do We Know But Live Like We Don't

When you start saving and start the process toward buying your home, that's when the belief that it is possible kicks in—and you say, No turning back. Because now it's your dream, and you will get it because you prayed for help from God. But now you must focus on the steps to get there—step one, step two, step three, and all the way to the end—that started the journey to get a home.

We always start with the end in mind.

Seasons

We can wish until we get blue in the face—spring must end for summer to begin.

We cannot take winter into summer or spring into fall. Seasons come and seasons go—we must live with them by adjusting. Mentally, it's a small adjustment because you have no choice. When you were an infant, someone did the adjustment for you.

As we live our lives, changes must happen—and we flawlessly adjust. As infants, we did infant things. As a child, I did childish things. As teens, we did crazy things. As adults, we must do adult things. Life dictates the seasons of our lives.

As we live life, our lives change. As infants, we did infant things. As a child, I did childish things. As teens, we did teen things—because life dictates what we do in that season. After graduating from high school, you are now embarking on adult living—where you must find a mate, prepare for the future, and watch the cycle of your own children adjust to the seasons.

I truly believe that everything begins with the end in mind.

Chapter Four: Learn to Listen So You Listen to Learn

I will learn to listen to God always, listening is for one respect. Listen to learn, so you learn from listening. You know that listening to someone makes them feel heard. Listening is not just hearing the person; it's really hearing what they are saying, and it shows you have empathy and are concerned about what you hear them say.

A young man I knew from Newark, New Jersey, knew the bible so well that every time someone spoke to him, he was always ready with a bible verse. No matter what the conversation was, he was always so ready; he literally can tell you there was a period there, that is Paul speaking, and that's Mathew. He was an accountant.

Bro, we're talking about you going to another city and staying focused. Nothing wrong with the bible verses, but stay on topic. When you are a know-it-all, you listen to give your thoughts, not to respond to what they say.

Sometimes someone can hear you while not listening to you because they are just waiting to not hear your voice, or waiting for you to STOP so they can say what they were thinking. That's why the phrase (sorry for interrupting you) is used when they want you to finish your thought. You were speaking during the conversation. But you could have just let me.

Why Do We Know But Live Like We Don't

Sometimes they are just waiting to have something better than what they heard, not knowing that the person might be at their lowest at that time, and that's their best

Why outdo them? Just listen and care.

When you truly listen to someone, you can hear more than they are saying. Sometimes you can feel what they are saying.

The Phrase, when people tell you who they are, believe them the first time. Listen to learn.

In school, you must listen to learn. Your goal is to move on and keep learning. You must listen to learn. Trust me, I tried it the other way and did the seventh grade twice. No Bueno, some do not listen to their teachers but pay very close attention to their boss.

But if you did listen to your teachers, you would have been the boss.

Prospective

Why do we know but live like we don't? We know we are not the same; all of us were born with different builds, we do not think the same, and we do not eat the same. Our fingerprints are different because we are different.

Sometimes we insist that others understand our point of view. Sometimes they can't; they just simply can never be in your shoes.

We want people to accept us, but we don't accept them the way they are, knowing they are not us.

Some people will jump out of a perfectly good airplane for fun... I would not.

Some people will bungee jump and zipline and scream the whole way just because.... I will not.

Some people eat frogs, squirrels, and snakes... I will not.

Why Do We Know But Live Like We Don't

That does not make the person jumping out of the plane crazy. That person might be thinking how crazy you are for not doing it.

The person bungee jumping and zip lining is not on a death wish; they just like the adrenaline rush that they get from doing that. They say it's like a roller coaster... I beg to differ.

Someone may look at the bungee jump setup and see disaster. Boy, that rope is going to snap with me, the harness is not going to fit right, I am going to slip out, something is going to go wrong.

If you think like that… do not do it.

The Bible tells us to speak what we want, ask, and it will be given; we have even heard as a man thinketh so is he. That makes us all individuals.

The next guy may walk up thinking they are professionals, they know what they are doing, plus they have people's lives at stake, and they have been doing this for years. Let's go!!

Then there is this guy. I have been thinking about this for a while. I really want to do this; they are professionals, and they know what they are doing. I haven't heard of any accidents. The weather is perfect, but I am scared. They get stuck in analysis paralysis and never face their fear.

Again, there is nothing wrong with either person's view; it can be just how they are made. We are all entitled to our own perspective, opinion, or point of view.

I mention that I would not eat frogs, snakes, elk, squirrels, or alligators, not that I think it is gross, but because I don't.

God said it is good to eat, and he also gave a choice to eat or not to eat.

But wait, I eat cows, goats, chickens, fish, and sharks. The squirrel eater might say I ain't eating no chicken and the family eating the elk could say that the cow can't come close to the taste of elk. Who am I to argue with any of them?

Prospective and opinions are the same; they are yours and you can keep them … or share them, and we must remember to give the other person the right to receive or reject your opinion.

That's funny, I know many people who would chastise you for eating pork chops and chitins, I mean, really get into you, but then turn around and eat bacon. They would say it's not pork, it's bacon.

Sometimes, when you make your point and it's understood, others will lean in your direction.

My son always stuck to his opinion because he believed it. He always wanted you to at least take a good look at his perspective. Honestly, I believe that is what makes him successful, just the way he says what he wants you to consider. He runs his own construction company. Proud, proud, very proud of him.

Well, he had a perspective on a brand of car while I was car hunting. He would say, Dad, do not even go in the lot that has that brand of car. And man, there were a few models that we loved, I mean, really loved. The brand made some very nice cars. He and I used to drive out to my jobs when he was younger, no wife and kids yet, he always says, when I get my family, I am going to keep them safe, I would never put them in one of those. I always shrug it off, thinking that's a great opinion to have about your future family.

But as the years went by, I was in my head, thinking I was passing the torch / getting ready to retire. We were driving to his job, yes, I loved working with and for my son. Anyway, he had a wife and a son of his own, and still said my family would not ride in that brand of car.

And as Dad, I say, Why do you always say that??

His reply was so simple, he said, Look and see what's involved in most accidents, 6 out of 10, that brand was involved.

Within that week, going to work, we saw a few fender benders and some highway accidents. I must admit 6 out of 10 that the brand was a part of the bump and grind.

He formulated his opinion, and it stayed with him that he could share it. Believe me, he believes it to his core. And live by HIS perspective.

I just think the brand manufactures so many cars, the odds are that it would happen.

Average not me

Why do we know but live like we don't?? I want to explain how I see the average.

- Draw a line at the end of the line, write the word average
- At the bottom of the line in the middle, you write best
- At the top of the line in the middle, you write worst
- Then you draw a line down from the word best
- Then you draw a line from the word worst
- At the bottom of the line, from best, you write worst
- At the top of the line, from worst, you write best

When you get it, you will never say you are average

Average = best of the worst and worst of the best.

Change the words if you want, but average is just that, average, middle of the road.

I remembered as a young person, about 16 or 17, I was 5,11 and was very happy to say I am of average height. Because others were 6 feet or something, or 5,6 to 5,10, that made me feel special.

I would dominate the 5,6 to 5,10 but get dominated by the 6, something, my God, that made me feel average.

But I can jump higher than most of the 6, something, and all of the 5,6 to 5,10s. I was not average there, and on top of that, I can shoot better than all the heights that were above average, so I stayed focused on what I was not average at.

Around that time, I did not care to say I was average because it then became a disadvantage. My mentality was that I am not average. I am me. Unique in my own way, even way above average. Because I was made in the image of God.

My son always says he believes he can beat any team he faces. He had this self-confidence that would scare most, but I believe my Non-average attitude rubbed off on him; he lived that way, knowing he was better than most, and he practiced more than most.

Imagine pitching a no-hitter at the age of 11 and hitting a home run in that game to win. Think of how big his head could have been. But his mother and I would always tell him it's because he practices more than the rest, and he understands the game differently, which he did.

In basketball, he and I would practice a few days before the games just to get him ready.

In one game, he was to play against a senior varsity player that has already determined which college he was going to play for. So, in the promotion for the game, they only mention that he was going to play against my son's school; they did not even mention my son as a player. I knew this was going to be good because I know my son very well. All I had to say was he is playing against your school, I hope you are IN that game. Honestly, all he said was hmm.

The night of the game, I remembered my son being nervous because, like he said, I had been dreaming about this game for weeks. I AM READY!!.

He almost broke the three-point record, as his father knew what he was capable of, but not like that, I think 32 points, and I know he did not feel average. They did not let him feel average; his school was chanting his name and celebrating the victory.

Average is a state of mind that I believe we can adjust to when we want it badly enough.

Chapter Five: Time and Timing

Why do we know but live like we don't?

We have said or have heard that God's timing is perfect, and if you are over the age of 30 with or without kids, you know that is real. When we ask God for patience, he gives us things to allow us to work on patience.

If we have a deadline and something must be done, we panic, and even worse, we start to worry, which stresses us out. In the good book, it says, DO NOT WORRY, for which one of us gains an extra minute of life because we worry about anything. Worrying to me is thinking of a solution that you do not believe would help, but you keep thinking of that same solution that you know will not work. Worrying only makes you tired. Tired of not solving the problem, when you know the things you can control, you control them to the best of your ability. And the things you cannot control, you leave to God.

Life will always be lifeing, seasons will change, and we all must get older. If you believe properly, you will not worry about anything.

Some of us worry because we believe it's up to us to solve. Just imagine if you are a parent and your child comes up to you and says, Dad/Mom, that bike we saw at the mall, I would love to have that. You, as a parent, are thinking I will get him /her that bike for his birthday, which is only weeks away. My God, he/she is going to love it.

God has blessed us; money is not a problem in your mind. You are thinking I could go get it today, but his/her birthday is only days away. I'll get it then in a few days. Your son/daughter walks away, and you hear them say in a grumbling way (I'll ask uncle because I don't know if they will get it.)

I believe that's what we do to God after we pray and ask God for it, but then try to figure it out on our own. And yes, I said try because you can't try.. We are to trust in what we recite. If we can say to someone to their face, God's timing is perfect, we'd better believe what we are saying.

The old phrase is "practice what you preach.

Don't say the book says, a Man should leave his father's and mother's home and find a wife, which is a good thing. But live in your parents' home until you are 40. I do not believe that is God's timing; it's yours.

With God, ALL things are possible. You can say you are with God, but if your heart is not, it will never work.

Yes, with the help of God, ALL things are possible.

You know all of us have only 24 hours in each day. How are we using them? We can't even cheat and steal more time in a day. 24, that's it.

The poor have 24, the mental middle class has 24, and the rich, to really rich, have 24.

No matter where you fit in, it's 24 hours. IN your day.

Career

Why do we know but live like we don't?

Each and every one of us, from the time we understand money and its proper use, starts thinking differently.

We seek out hustle that we believe would put us in the best position to accomplish our dreams and goals. We focus on getting to the next level from high school or college, which, to me, is perfect timing by God, the change from one season to the next season to carry on.

Most will continue to climb the imaginary ladder because they want more and more. Again, nothing wrong with that. But how do you prepare to stop working/retire to enjoy your golden years?

I am starting a bit late for some, but I believe that God's timing is perfect.

There are so many ways that God shows us His ways are not our ways, but when He shows us, we must trust and believe.

I believe that's why He shows and allows us to have vision and dreams in our renewed mind, and we always pray that we will be ready to do what we believe God's will is in our lives.

When I started to believe with my whole heart, I saw and lived the difference. For me, it was like night and day.

Trust and believe with your whole heart. Your whole heart, not 3/4 or 1/2, ALL.

We know that what we do as our hustle will pay our bills for most, that's 4 to 8 hours a day. I believe that leaves you with 4 hours to practice consistency, focus, determination, motivation, and I will finish what I start. That mixture puts you in a great position.

I believe that gives you a shot at a different lifestyle.

A very good friend of mine said to me, What you do during the day, pay your bills, and what you do before you go to sleep, gives you a lifestyle. You can watch TV or do something to improve yourself.

Then he hit me with You look at me and I am rich and live great, but you have the same amount of hours in a day that I have, only 24 for everyone. Then it starts over.

Then he said, I did some things I did not really care to do for a little while to establish the resources to invest in my dream. And he clarified by saying, Nothing illegal.

I worked for a company that told me what they thought I was worth, and I had to take what they believed I was worth until I could change it by following my visions/dreams.

All that he said to me bothered me because I knew that I knew how to do that.

I know the best investment is self-investment.

The thing is, why do I know but live like I don't??

Financial understanding

Why do we know but live like we don't??

We have all heard that money is the root of evil. The truth is, the love of money is the root of all evil. We need money to live. We need money to get medication. We need money for almost everything. It is how we put money in our minds that dictates how we see money.

I need to get that piece of land, and I need to get that car with no car payments. I need to get that house with no mortgage.

Too worried about my finances because I did not plan properly. I personally do not like to worry about money.

The word says I took care of the birds, I took care of the lilies of the field, and how much more important are you?

For two years, I had the same problem: I couldn't spend more than $20 on my grandkids. Why did I not prepare for the following year?? Why couldn't I save to do better??

I realize I have changed nothing, so I should not expect anything to change. Everything remains the same if not changed. Well, I changed something, and things change. What did I change, you ask??

I renewed my mind

The same mind that got you here can not be the same mind to gets you out.

I planned and scheduled my bills to maximize my outcome. I understand what I brought in and what needs to go out. I figured if what I brought was not enough, then I must shut off the TV.

With a renewed mind, you must ask God for help because it's a new mind you do not understand yet. Ask and it will be given to you. Knock and the doors will be open, is the mentality that a renewed mind allows you to practice… And live by.

All of us know how to plan our finances and practice what we preach, so we must focus and do it. We know better than we do.

Physical and health

Why do we know but live like we don't??

Our plan is to change our lives, always for the better. We want good finance, and we also need to stay alive to enjoy our wealth. The plan is to focus on building wealth so that money is not a problem. And to live so you enjoy your effort. Walking, light exercising, cutting back on sugar and salt, live like you know you must live. Very doable.

Remember, if you think you can, you will, and at this point, you know you can.

Putting your finances together requires Dedication, Determination, Consistency, and I know I can do this because I need to and I will. Mentality

While getting your money right, you start feeling good about your accomplishments, then you can say to yourself I feel good about my finances.

If I could add physical fitness to that equation. You start walking and thinking differently. Boy, this feels good, not worrying about money, and I am exercising to live better.

When you look good and feel good, you do good. We change our diet to match physical activity, eating better, reading food labels ... avoiding too much sugar, too much salt. And good antioxidants are great, you look to see if it has vitamin B12 and C.

We are mentally and physically strong with good health. We received all of that because we were willing to invest in and dedicate the right effort to you.

You made up your mind to change you, just that little bit. And you became determined to stay consistent with your plans and goals. I do not want to make money and spend it all on something I could fix in the journey.

A renewed mind should be a balanced mind.

Chapter Six: Family and Relationship

Why do we know but live like we don't?

Family means the world to me, the togetherness, the love, the knowing that they have your back. I am from a big family, 9 kids, 3 girls, and 6 boys. Being the second child, the first son is awesome. I always felt like I must lead. I always wanted my Dad to be proud of me.

But I was a typical young boy into everything, and I thank God for the whippings I got to keep me in line.

Amazing, my Dad would say before that *sass whooping I do not like doing this to you, but I believe if I did not, you would get worse. He was right because whenever I was in my mischievous mood, I would remember that leather belt across my thighs and stop.

My Dad did not say, as a matter of fact, I have never heard my Dad say I LOVE YOU to anyone. He did not say it, but he showed it every minute of his life.

For me, he showed me love by expecting me to be better than he was.

- He talks to me about my future and tells me he prays for me daily
- He made sure I never felt left out
- He started a business with Hopes of me taking over
- He did stuff like put us in the trunk of his car to get into the driving movies
- He taught me how to swim
- He never says I LOVE YOU, but I have felt LOVE my whole life

And hey, he did that for the other 8 as well.

My God, I miss him. Yes, he is dead, but I will continue to make him proud.

MOM / MISS RUTH

My Mom was the glue that kept us as a family. She would never let anyone or anything get between her family that she had built. She did not believe in breaking commitments. If she loves you, that's for life. If she dislikes you, that's also for life. I know of one young lady, from the time my Mom saw her, she disliked her. I mean

really dislike her.

She even has a story of a person she disliked since she was three years old.

I thank God He chose her to be the Mom for me.

My Mom loved her kids equally, yet differently. My Mom gave birth to 10 kids. Her first child was born when she was 16. Everything for her was the first. First love, first pregnancy, first baby, and first gagagogo love. No matter what, no other child could wear that love.

The second birth my Mom had, unfortunately, the baby passed when she was months old.

BUT the doctor told my Dad to get her pregnant again so she does not grieve too long.

That next baby was me, the only planned pregnancy (that's my story, and I am sticking to it). I was the first boy my Mom was pleased to give my Dad a son. Imagine the love I got as the first boy. No other child could wear that love.

My parents lived where they needed proper papers to work, and if she got pregnant, that could buy them time. That child gave my Mom and Dad some breathing room. That child was the first to be born there. They were in love with her. No one else could wear that love.

They got to the point that they could travel because they had the proper papers. Mom was pregnant, but not close to the due date; she could be back to have the baby. The baby was born premature, while on vacation, she was ok, just premature. The time came for them to return, and the doctor said to Mom, It's on you if something happens to the child. Mom protected her with everything she had. The protective, premature, motherly love. No other child can wear that love.

The other baby was a son. They were happy to get another son because it was me and three girls, so they wanted to break it up. The child reminded Mom of her side of the family. He got the lips, the hair, the light complexion. No other child could wear that love.

Mom always says she wants more kids. This time, Dad, the head of the home, just realized he could give his full name to a child, so they prayed for a boy. They got their prayers answered. He walks like Dad, he talks like Dad, he fishes like Dad, he swims like Dad. Well, he was named after Dad.

And Mom, those were Mom's words. She helped him accomplish something as simple as naming your child after you... That Love no one else can wear.

Mom and Dad always do things with us, driving to movies, picnicking on the beach all day, and watching lots of karate movies.

So the next child, they wanted to name him after one of them. The Karate star.

Again, they prayed for a boy. When he was born, I would hear them say he got that round face like the Chinese people, LOL. That child was always happy and kept us all in stitches, especially Mom. My goodness, he is funny. No other child could wear that love.

Dad was getting his fishing business off the ground, and we were doing a little better because we did not have to buy fish ever again. We had a better TV, and we were watching better shows. Marcus Welby, M.D., for example

They were going to get a good doctor name; they did not care if it was a boy or a girl, it was going to have a doctor name. The name they chose, to me, is perfect for what they wanted to do, hmm. (he married a doctor.) That love only he can wear.

The last child. Mom would say my scraping because they knew that was it, no more. She said she was going to give it all she had left; she did, what a mighty man.

He is. Loved by ALL and he loves you right back just the same. They used all the knowledge and experience from all the other children, and knowing that's it.

No other child could wear that love.

We knew she loved us because she showed it daily. There were two people who were going to go through any and everything to make their family work. Mom always says she knows her role, and he knows his.

Mom and Dad's relationship was built on LOVE, RESPECT for the head of the house, and TRUST.

Dad went home on June 29, 2017.

Mom went home on June 23, 2023.

To God be all the glory.

Ricky Barton

Chapter Seven: Wisdom, Knowledge, and Understanding

Why do we know but live like we don't?

We know that wisdom is what you seek; most go on to college seeking wisdom. Some trade school and some military. We are always seeking to be better than we were yesterday. The good book said, Seek and you will find.

Will find what I was stuck on. If you seek it, you will find it.

In the good book, the richest man only wanted wisdom. Because when you have the wisdom of anything, it's yours to keep, and one cannot take it away from you. Your wisdom should guide you, because better wisdom, I believe, means better decisions we should make.

When we seek wisdom and we find it, we can now say we have Knowledge of that. Knowledge is what you gain after you find wisdom. The knowledge that you gain is also yours and yours to keep. What you do with your knowledge is entirely up to you, I truly believe that.

We have heard that knowledge is power; that is true if you choose to use it right.

One can have knowledge of: writing, reading, drawing, dancing, playing a sport, driving, and even taking a picture.

Knowledge of those few mentioned has put someone in a position to live where money is not one of their problems. Knowledge really is power when you understand how to use it. The understanding of the knowledge you have that no one can take from you will make you feel and think powerful. Because you seek wisdom with the end in mind to get better. You found

Knowledge of how to be better, now you know better, you do better.

Your understanding of your life is different because of your renewed mind. If what you practice is what you become, then I will practice like the big boys: MJ, LJ, KB, LT, SBsr, even my grand nephew lil WILL.

We admire them because of how they practice behind closed doors. They seek all the wisdom of their field, and get to know it well, and their understanding of it gives them a better life.

Remember, wisdom is what you seek, knowledge is what you get, and understanding is how you use what you got.

As I am looking in the mirror, I say to myself, I don't know about you, but I am going to seek wisdom, knowledge, and understanding.

While I am seeking the Kingdom of God.

To God be all the Glory

Something or nothing

Why do we know but live like we don't??

As a foreman of a roofing company, I had many crew members, so I've had lots of conversations.

I've heard: I need a better job, I must lose weight, I need to buy a house, I wish I could get my own company.

Every one of those conversations was heartfelt because they meant it and really wanted it.

We even started a savings game just to give us a push. We got to a point where we realized we said the same thing last year. Come to think of it, we've been saying the same thing for the past 5 years.

Damn, that hit me hard because it was as simple as we did NOT change anything, so nothing was going to change.

Some of the same guys were still around.

And guess how we sounded 5 years later; I need a new job, I need to lose weight, I need to buy a house, and I wish I could get my own company.

Then one by one we changed something, and we couldn't believe it, something had changed.

One of the assistant foremen kept saying, I don't know what I am afraid of, but I am afraid to make that move. With the baby coming, I know I need to find more room. But with the baby coming, I can't risk it. My goodness, my apartment is too small now. But I cannot afford to move. My car is falling apart, but these car prices.

For one, he is afraid of the unknown; it is unknown, HE DOESN'T KNOW what he is AFRAID of. He knew his problem, but he kept talking himself out of it. Eventually, he put one foot in front of the other, and he changed his thinking as a man thinks so is he.

Speak what you want, not what you don't want.

He lives in a very beautiful home and owns some rentals. He drives a very nice blue truck.

I am a firm believer that if you do nothing, you should expect nothing. If you do something, something will happen. If you change something, something will change.

Lean not on your own understanding.

Because you say: With God all things are possible

With God!!

God's way is not our way. You think you will get a red car. God gave you a Blue car, answered prayer, just not your understanding

Chapter Eight: Minor Adjustment

Why do we know but live like we don't?

It's not every morning you wake up and feel energized and ready to go. But you have a hustle to go to. Because you have a home and a car and, to top it off, you like to eat.

How do you go from *being too tired to even getting out of bed? Good morning! Yeah, two titi bread, a bun, cheese, and some bush tea?*

There is so much that, if well planned, you can build momentum for your day. Let's start with being grateful we woke up.

Then God made it so that you had to pee, you must get up to pay that some attention. He made you yawn while in the bathroom. Oh, that breath as you are peeing, You are looking at your toothbrush. All of this was done with you being half awake.

Your momentum has started, and you are doing things without thinking.
That's the hands of God getting you started, Even before you are awake. God has protective angels encamped around you.

And sometimes we believe we can help God by sleeping with a knife or a weapon under our pillow… why?? God's angels have weapons you can't imagine. That's why He says *No weapon formed against me shall prosper.*

Our routine that we follow every morning starts with us not even being fully coherent. We should be thankful that He ordained you to be you and only you.

Then He let you be you—the one that is supposed.to seek first the Kingdom of God and His righteousness,The one that is supposed to praise and worship Him, The one who is to pray without ceasing.

Yes, the one who knows that it's His will that will be done.

For me, those adjustments out of order made it tough because I was praying without ceasing.Then I would praise and worship and follow the Sabbath.I was doing what was said to do, but skipped the thing He said to do FIRST:*Seek ye first the kingdom of God and His righteousness.*

My morning routine, after God allows me to be fully awake:I thank God for giving me another day.I pray and ask Him, *What do You want from me on this day?*I listen to praise music that reminds me that with God, ALL things are possible,Songs that say words like *God, You have done it again. I am next in line for my blessing. Taste and see that our Lord is good.*

And if you see my life, I so-so wonder. But if you know my God, He is a miracle worker.

My playlist is big and encouraging… Try Jah Love, A chapter a day keeps the devil away, Jah is standing by my side, so why should I be afraid?The words of those songs help me adjust my mind that I want to renew.

God starts you off in the a.m., then He allows you to do your part until you go to sleep, and His angels take over.He allows us to be us: He leads us beside quiet waters and green pastures.

Then it is up to us to drink from the water, rest by the water, bathe in the water, or swim in the water.He leads us, and we make the choices that we believe are part of His will.

Why Do We Know But Live Like We Don't

Thinking of how one of my grandsons adjusted to daycare, something he has no idea about.He would cry and say, *Papa, I don't want to go,* and as he cried, my eyes started to sweat.

My God, I love them so much.

His going to daycare the first week was tough for me and me. I adjusted because I had to, plus I wanted no one to see my eyes sweat.Also, because of the attachments/bond we had.

But for him, he was crying because everything was new to him and unknown. As the weeks went on, his cries stopped, and he was almost eager to go to daycare. I had to adjust to not having him around all day.

That was because from the first day my son said, *He needs sunlight, and you have it perfect in our prayer room.* Then he took off the five-day-old baby's onesie and handed him to me. I am still melting. He loves his papa.

But he had to adjust because the news was coming. I kinda like this. Other people my age did the same things I do. I love Papa, but he is Papa, and my new friends are nice, and they like me too.

His younger brother, when he was only two days old, the doctors wanted to take his blood, and up to now, my eyes swell just thinking of that. My adjustment was not to watch what they had to do. Now, to see him ride his balancing bike makes my eyes sweat again. Look at how much we've adjusted.

His mom would have him say the letters of the alphabet, so I would test him and call a B a C. He would say so gently, *Papa, no, that's not a B, okay, that's a C.*

Every vision and thought I have of them is that I pray that my prayers will be answered in their life. To see him make the adjustments to anything that came at him, to me, is amazing, how God's will will be done.

Thinking of how many adjustments we must make made me reminisce about another adjustment. Like my son becoming a dad for the first time. He knew the inches the fetus would be every day. He would say to me, *Dad, it's a pear size this week.*

He knew what his wife must and must not eat. He and his wife watched YouTube to learn all they could to be the best parents they could be.

They went to church more, and they changed without seeing how they changed. Watching my son made me very proud to see how he took the little he learned from me. To become a dad that others would love to have.

Both my son and grandsons adjusted so much. We did not even talk about what his wife had to adjust to. Her nine-month body, mind, and emotions adjustment… But God. They are now the praying family. Our prayers will continue.

From my great-grandmother to my mom and dad to me. Now they will teach their children to pray. To God be all the glory.

My grandmother prayed for me, and I can see how they answered in my life. Accumulation of many minor adjustments made the difference.

Give God something to bless

Why do we know but live like we don't? It is so easy to say, *God gave me this gift, and I thank Him every day.*

What is your gift? How are you using your gifts? Who is being blessed by your gifts?

We tend to see those answered in others. Seems as though, I believe it, but not for me.

My sister—well, to me, she is just blessed. She went to college to study pharmacy and, upon completion, She gravitated to education. I believe education is her gift. She even skipped a grade. I'll say it again: she skipped a grade.

She uses her gifts to teach and shape young lives. Have you ever talked to her? All she talks about is the young people she shares her gifts with. Without thinking, she answered the three questions: Gift—education, she uses her gift to teach, and blessing—young lives.

I could have said, look at athletics, a basketball player's gifts that God gave him, he uses his gift to entertain, and all of us who enjoy benefit from their use of their gifts.

Actors, doctors, mothers, fathers, police, construction, and pastors are all some common overlooked built-in gifts. Yes, mom and dad—some dads raise their kids, they coach them, allow them to excel to the top of the sports they play. Mom allowing dad to be the example for the boys, and dad allowing her to teach his daughter to be a woman, causes her to be able to do that.

Do your best with what God gave. I believe every day we must give God something to bless.

Chapter Nine: Permission to Start

Why do we know but live like we don't?

We know that anyone can start anything. We start school, friendships, hustles, ideas, and relationships. Starting should not over-impress anyone—be happy and glad that they or you started.

We get started because we imagine what the end results would be.

We get motivated in our minds because of dreams and the thirst for more.

Then some get determined to go for it—that's when your heart is involved.

You think of the results you want and the work needed.These things must happen in order for me to accomplish my dreams.Then your mind and heart know we must add consistency.Because VICTORY is in the COMPLETION.

The perseverance you must endure—how much are you willing to give to YOU?You cannot get 100% out of anything you are not willing to give 100%.Hence the phrase: *You get what you give.*You give nothing, you should expect absolutely nothing.

Once you say *I don't know?* You are seeking a reason not to do it.The thing is, you DO know. You know if you think you can, you will.If you think you can't, you won't.

There are times others want it for you more than you want it for yourself.That's when you must be honest with yourself and with those who believe in you.Ask yourself: *If every decision I've made up to now has me right where I put myself, then why would I choose that one?*

Ever hear *If I knew back then what I know now! Boy, I would have...*Pump your brakes. Hey, this is now, and you know, so boy, you should…So you have the knowledge you wish you had back then.What would you have done with the knowledge you have now, back then?

Sometimes you do not know what you would have done.Because the ideas that you have now are new ideas, from your growth.You were not thinking like this back then.

We must find a way to understand that our ideas only make sense to us and not anyone else, also because it's your idea.Most of the time, they believe they are helping you avoid getting hurt.Hurt from what? Not all investments are winners, but you never stop seeking the end in mind.

Let the only person who learned to ride a bike and never fell at least once, please stand up.

How could they understand the dreams that God put in you?If God ordained you to be you and only you, and He put that dream in you, then how do you expect anyone to understand?

It's amazing that we all would say we are different, but we expect someone to understand our differences.*Lean not on your own understanding*... your understanding of your idea God put in you.They will never understand you. If you can't lean on your understanding, how can they lean on your understanding???

We all get to a place in life that we say *IF IT'S TO BE, IT'S UP TO ME and God only.* That's when you think of the one-rabbit scenario and focus on finishing your task.

I was once in a multi-level marketing business, a very successful business. When they showed the plan, I saw the dream. They helped me see the end: the house, the cars, the vacation, and the great life. The whole system was great. It was great before me and will continue to be great after me. Very well put-together business systems.

I watched as others did what they were supposed to do and achieved much success. My mentor at that time continued to tell me how much he believed in me. He believed in me to give it my best 100%. I also believed in myself, but I was not as committed as he believed.

You see, he believed I was going to give my whole heart to the business. I only wanted to give half of my heart to the business. Because I had my own business that I was now thinking I must split my time with.

My mentor even said, *I am giving you permission to start your next-level journey.* He was giving me permission, but I wasn't giving it myself.

When I did not move up, he asked me, *Do you know why?* And walked away. I did not permit myself to be what I knew I could be.

Anyone can start, but only a few would finish—and finish right. The few that do know what made the difference. Anyone can start; it's the finish that's impressive.

Leaving it

We are to ask for help and accept the help, then use the help. As a child, I knew my mom and dad would do just about anything for their family. My mom would go hungry to make sure we ate. My dad would cry when he couldn't do any more for us.

Mom and Dad were not the type to ask outsiders for help, even family. Dad always thought outsiders only bring trouble and pick what they want to help with—that only benefits them. They both would say, *We will do our best and pray God Almighty would do the rest.*

Sometimes we must make a decision to leave it to God, and when we leave it, we really leave it.

When God put me through something I never thought would happen to me, and then He said, *Do you trust me?* If you really trust me, ALLOW me to be the God you talk about.

Man, the enemy wanted me to lose my identity, my years of dedication to my family, my military benefits, my house, my car, my tools, my fruit trees, and my life—everything. But God said these things must happen in order for you to do my will. He said, *Follow the basic instructions before leaving this earth.*

That's when I heard, Leave it at the altar and let God do the alterations.

When I look back, I am truly glad God allowed me to leave the things that were not for me behind.

I am grateful for what God has done for me. I see all the blessings and answered prayers, down to prayers that I prayed for over 30 years.

I see our God Almighty answering them. God's timing is perfect. And we all know God blesses everyone who seeks Him and believes in Him.

To God be all the glory.

Because of what He has done, I am ready for my next season, new chapter, renewed mind, minor adjustments, And the new me that came out of the smoke.

The new me will be what God wants me to be.

Chapter Ten: You Really Do Know

Because you know this

We are to be better than we were yesterday. We should always remind ourselves: *Why do we know but live like we don't?* Because you know this, you can't unknow it. Because you know this, you will make different decisions to shape your life. Because you know this, you must practice and practice to become better at what you practice. And because you know wrong from right, we should live accordingly.

Mentality

As a man thinketh, so is he. So, what are you thinking? We want a renewed mind to think differently. We see things in a new way because we know better. We eat differently because we know better. We talk differently because the old way kept us back. Speak what you want.

We know we can't *try* to do or not do. Because if you think you can, you will. And if you think you can't, you will not. We have to practice renewing our own minds. We become better at what we practice.

Better planning is needed in your renewed mind. They say if you do not plan, then you plan to fail. **No one** wants to fail.

Believing

To believe in yourself is the key to anything you want to accomplish. If you can't believe in yourself, who should?

When we trust God, we must believe He has equipped us with all we need to accomplish the desires of our hearts. He put them there.

Believing in yourself brings the confidence that is needed. Believing in you pulls your focus.

If you are hungry not just for food but hungry for change in you:

- Believe in you
- Focus on you
- Dedicate your time to yourself
- Become consistent with you
- Motivate you

You must do these things because you have the end in mind. As you work on yourself, you will change. Accept it—you must.

Remember, if you change something, something will change. Seasons come and seasons go.

Listening

If we are going to listen, we must listen to learn. Do not listen to remember selective sections of the conversation. Give that person the respect to hear what they thought was something they wanted to say to you.

Replying to the conversation should only be based on the conversation, not on how much you hate your job. Giving your perspective should only be if they ask for it.

If you are not married, do not give advice on marriage, because that's your perspective and not your experience. A man could never give menstrual advice because he never had one. But over the years, having your daughter and listening to her, you learn how to help her and what to give her. None of this could have happened without you listening to mom, sisters, and your daughter.

One of my clients was working with paper all day and on the phone. She hired me to do a job. She explained what she wanted, and I was off to do the job. I have been in construction for over 20 years. What she wanted was basic, average work. I said average because the above average comes after the base.

As I was laying out the base, she came and screamed, *Not like that!!* "What do you mean?" I asked. She said, *It has to go like this...* I allowed her to finish her explanation.

And I said, "I have built many of what you are asking for, and most of what you are asking for is at the end."

She got really upset, and as she was leaving and slamming the door, she grumbled, *I don't think he knows what he is doing.* Then texted me, *I will get someone else to get it done.*

I swallowed my pride and texted her: You gave me a deposit, and I have materials here. I'll put it together and will remove it if you do not like it.

She got home from work and said, *That's exactly what I wanted.*

She hired me because she heard people say, *He did that job.* She personally saw some of my jobs. She gave me money and signed our agreement. She even talked about future jobs.

Time and timing

We always say God's timing is perfect, and with God, all things are possible.

Then we get upset when things do not happen when we want them to.

We, to me, are confusing ourselves because we say one thing and do the other.

A mentor of mine said that it is crazy.

He said, You say God's timing is perfect with conviction, and your demeanor looks like you believe what you are saying.

But your action shows you do not really believe what you said.

A young lady I knew. She knew all the right things to say, she studied the bible just to say the right things, but her actions were so far from what she was saying.

We would hear the chatter in the back. Girl, take your own advice and get right before you try to help anyone

I truly believe she meant well, but was putting the horse behind the cart.

She had trouble with her dad, but felt ok to tell others. Honor your mom and father when she couldn't

She always wanted to get married, but never left the house to seek and find a husband.

She was very smart, but the right people will not know because she only talks to people she believes are below her.

I really pray she gets what's hers because she deserves it.

My advice to her is to believe with your whole heart and trust that God will give you what you want at the right time.

Keep your head up, and know what's yours will always be yours. God got you.

Do your best with what God gave you.

Relationship and Family

Reading the Bible speaks so much about family and relationships: Adam and Eve, Samson and Delilah, Abraham and Sarah, Patriarch and Matriarch, Isaac and Rebekah, Boaz and Ruth, Joseph and Mary, Zechariah and Elizabeth, and Aquila and Priscilla (they were tent makers).

Adam and Eve—we know the story. Samson and Delilah—we know that story. Boaz and Ruth—we know their stories.

The relationships between the couples are all different and gave different examples. My understanding is they knew their roles, no matter what it was.

- Adam and Eve—she opened the doors of sin.
- Samson and Delilah—showed betrayal and how people close to you can hurt you.
- Boaz and Ruth—showed how to trust in God and wait on the Lord.
- Joseph and Mary—showed how to obey God and believe what He says.

In today's family and relationships, some women turn the kids against the man who raised them. Some kick out fathers who were there for their family for their whole life. 40 years of sacrifice mean nothing to some of these women. I am not bashing women.

The man can buy a house and have no payments, buy a car with no payments, everything he believes God wants him to do—but it was not enough. So betrayal is the answer to some.

Like Samson, he asked, *What did I do to deserve this?* And that's when you remember God's ways are not our ways, and we cannot change that.

- God's way—Eve, do not eat the apple.
- God's way—Delilah would not cut his hair.
- God's way—a man is the head of his house, especially if God allows him to provide and protect his family. Don't throw him out and try to replace him with a homeless person, because I will never believe that's God's will.

The devil wins when he can split up what God put together.God gave Adam and Eve to help him, not to destroy him.Samson chose Delilah to be with her, not for her to destroy him.

God created a family: Jesus had a family on earth.

Wisdom, Knowledge, and Understanding

Wisdom is what you seek.Knowledge is what you gain from seeking.Understanding is how you use what you seek and gain to help others.

You know you are blessed to be a blessing.

The mission in life is to seek and find wisdom

Collect and own knowledge

Use and benefit from your understanding

Adjustments

We know life is a series of adjustments we must make to others,

We must adjust to our own growth

We must adjust to our hustle

As we get older, our eyesight changes, and we get glasses

All minor adjustments.

Believe with all your heart.

Romans 10:9 Trust in the Lord with all your heart — *Proverbs 3:5* Speak what you want — *Mark 11:24* Seek and you will find — *Matthew 7:7-8* Lean not on your own understanding — *Proverbs 3:5-6* Ask and it will be given — *Matthew 7:7* You have not because you ask not — *James 4:2* He is the truth and the light — *John 14:6* I will listen to the Lord — *Psalm 85:8* It is His will that will be done — *Matthew 6:10* You must believe — *Hebrews 11:6* Without faith it is impossible to please God — *Hebrews 11:6* God's ways are not our ways — *Isaiah 55:8-9* The people perish for lack of vision — *Proverbs 29:18* Let the weak say I am strong — *Joel 3:1* With God, all things are possible — *Matthew 19:26* Seek ye first the Kingdom of God — *Matthew 6:33* Give God something to bless — *Deuteronomy 15:10* Live the abundant life — *John 10:10* Pray without ceasing — *1 Thessalonians 5:17* I will praise my God with all my heart — *Psalm 86:12*